Publisher: PIAOTT Publishing and Graphic Design, Chicago, IL

My Sisters In Christ

Wilma Brumfield-Lofton and Shirley Rice

Printed in the United States of America

©2021 by Library of Congress Cataloging-in-Publication Data

ISBN: 978-1-7362522-4-6

Cover Photo: Ricardo Gomez Angel/unsplash.jpg

My Sisters In Christ

Author
Wilma Brumfield-Lofton

Co-Author
Shirley Rice

Words From the Authors

We were inspired to write this book because of all the wonderful Christian women that are in an organization that we both are members of called Wake Up To Praise. These women love the Lord as well as their families and others. You can always depend on them to pray for you, encourage, inspire, empower and lift you up! If you need a shoulder to cry on or a listening ear, someone is there. In this book are stories about women whose friends are like Sisters In Christ! Showing love, patience, kindness, forgiveness and keeping each other lifted in Prayer! Many of these women live in different states, but are always there for each other, only a phone call away to chat or help in times of need. These sisters are always around, if you are in the valley or celebrating accomplishments, special events, birthdays, anniversaries, etc. Showering you with love, motivational text messages, beautiful cards, gifts, etc. Sisters that are always there to laugh with you, walk with you, comfort you during difficult times and challenges in life. Blessings to all women who are like "My Sisters In Christ."

Table of Contents

Wilma 7, 9

Shirley 10

Adrienne 13

Amber 16

Annie 18

Audrey 19

Avis 20

Carolyn 22

Claudette 23

Cleopatra 27

Connie 30

Darcel 33

Denise B. 34

Denise M. 36

Joycelyn 38

Julia 40, 42

LaShonda 43

LaTasha 45

Laura 48

Lori 49

Louise 50

Mary G. 51

Mary S. 52

Nell 56

Sharon 59, 61, 62

Tawana 63

Virginia 64

Wanda 67

Thank You 68

"A sister is a gift to the heart, a friend to the spirit, a golden thread to the meaning of life."

Isadora James

Wilma Brumfield-Lofton

Wilma

wo of my best friends are Avis Price and Juanita Green. We met in church when we were in elementary school. We also were in choir together, we preformed in church plays and we were even baptized on the same day.

Our parents were good friends, so we visited each others homes and sometimes had sleepovers. We enjoyed going to movies, parties, shopping etc., always having each others best interest at heart. We are always there for each other with loving spirits and forgiving hearts through good times or bad times. We have shared many

Avis & Wilma

special occasions together such as birthdays, graduations, weddings, child-births, baby showers, etc. We have so many awesome memories! Now our children are all grown up, we live in different states, but we remain in touch with each other. We are members of "Wake Up To Praise" a group of Christian believers who meet on a conference call two times a week for prayer and bible study. I thank God for my amazing Sisters In Christ!

Juanita Green

Marietta Willie Wilma & Nona

Marietta Jordan, Willie Kellye, Nona Honeycutt and I were neighbors; although, Nona and I moved, the four of us stay in touch with each other by continuing to celebrate our birthdays and doing our monthly luncheons. Marietta makes the best Pasta Salad and Willie makes the best Tea Cakes, both are award winning!!! When we are together we have lots fun, good fellowship and delicious food! It is a blessing to have loyal friends who love the Lord and keep each other lifted in prayer! We are certainly Sisters In Christ!

Wilma Brumfield-Lofton

Terrie Peavy

My brother Michael Peavy and his wife Terrie have been married for over thirty years. They have five children and seven grandchildren whom they enjoy spending time with and all of the grandchildren love being at their grandparent's home. It is a blessing to have a sister-in-law who loves the Lord. Michael and Terrie both love talking about God's Word and sharing God's Good News with others!

My beloved grandmother Ruby Sims who was Blessed to live to the age of 105 years old, used to live in Chicago, Illinois. She was a person who loved God, her family and friends. When she was around 97 years old my brother and sister-in-law moved her to the Mt. Zion Pleasant View Plaza Senior Apartments in Hammond, Indiana so she would be closer to them and my mother. My precious grandmother enjoyed her apartment, fun activities, having lunch with her friends and attending Mount Zion M. B. Church under the teaching of Pastor William R. Collins.

When my grandmother turned 100 years old the staff in her apartment building gave her a big birthday celebration. Just before my grandmother turned 101 years old she had to have her foot amputated due to a injury, after the surgery my grandmother spent time in a rehab for seniors where she developed bedsores. Michael and Terrie decided to move my grandmother in with them where they nurtured and took excellent care of her. Under their care, the bedsores were healed and my grandmother looked great, happy and loved. I thank God for my dedicated and loving brother Michael and sister-in-law Terrie for being caregivers to my wonderful grandmother. Terrie is not only my sister-in-law but she is My Sister In Christ.

Shirley Rice

Shirley

My Sisters In Christ

Hello Sisters!

Julia Drove

Linda Hodges

In life, we never have a chance to decide who we want as our sisters. However, I have been very blessed to have three biological sisters and two first cousins, Clara and Frances that seemed more like our sisters than cousins. Yes, we did practically everything together. Because Julia was my youngest sister at the time, she could not hang with us; we all protected Julia. That is simply what big sisters do. By the time Linda was born, Julia was ten years old, and I am a junior in high school. We did not grow up together, and I missed most of her childhood memories. However, I recall buying her beautiful outfits and would read her bedtime stories. Even after I moved away, I never failed to be a blessing to my sisters.

Growing up, my older sisters and cousins loved to go running, taking long walks, and riding our bicycles. I can barely recall a time that we disagreed with one another. On the weekend, we would get our Bibles out and read scriptures. Then decide which scripture to learn to recite at church for "Baptist Youth Training Union" (BYTU). After graduation, many of us left our hometown, but we always kept in touch.

My sisters, cousins, and I grew closer as the years passed. We became best friends. We were devastated when our sister Regina suffered a stroke. She fought a good fight until the very end of her life.

Regina was Salutation of class. She went to college after graduation. Regina graduated from nursing school as a Licensed Practical Nurse (LPN) and furthered her career by returning to college and graduating with a degree in bookkeeping. She loved life and would light up the room with her bubbly personality. Regina always loved people and entertaining. She loved spending time with her two sons and two daughters, could sing like no other, and excelled in almost everything she put her mind to. Apart from her other accomplishments, she was an excellent cook. Everybody loved the meals that she prepared. I will always love and miss you dearly, my dear sister.

Wilma Brumfield-Lofton

Apart from my biological sisters, I have been very blessed to have several Sisters in Christ. One Sister in Christ that I have grown to love is Wilma Lofton. Wilma and I first met at church. She was always well reserved, always energetic, cheerful, and simply a joy to be around. We have so much in common. Our children grew up together and did practically everything together. Wilma and I remained very close friends long after our children grew up and married and had their own families. We have traveled and worked together at church and in sales. Our love for Christ deepened along the way. Although we now live in different states, it is as though we still live in the same state. I thank God for my friend and that she is a mighty woman of God.

Elizabeth "Liz" Campbell

My next friend and I met while singing together. We clicked right away. The thing about my friends is that our personalities are so much alike. Elizabeth Campbell, (Liz) for short, is full of fun, always cheerful, and the life of any party. She has a bubbly personality; she is an Evangelist, and her husband is a Minister. Liz loves to sing, praise, dance, and preach the word of God. We have traveled extensively together. We have shopped and shared recipes and cooked special dishes together. Liz can make a bread pudding and peach cobbler that would have you coming back for more.

Amazingly, each friend shares some of the same qualities. Both of my sisters in Christ are go-getters, excellent cooks, and have great family love. We laugh and joke around with each other and encourage and promote one another without ever falling out. These are my spiritual sisters that I met at church, and that bond has thrived down through the years.

If you are blessed to find that special friend, hold on tight and never let go. I thank God for all of my Sisters In Christ, for they too hold a special place in my heart.

Minister Adrienne D. Watson

Adrienne

My Wonderful Sister In Christ

When asked to identify and describe a Woman of God I consider to be my Sister in Christ, I did not have to think long and hard; but I had to choose one person over many viable candidates. This choice made it more of a process of elimination, which caused me to narrow it down to "one person." Again, I found myself scrambling to 'pick and choose' if you will, leaving others on the cutting floor. What it came down to eventually is this phenomenal woman in my life, who is not only a friend but one who epitomizes the life, the character, the soul, and spirit of a Christian woman and Sister in Christ. She embodies the spirit of Christ in her humility, her transparency, and her commitment to God and Christ. My Sister-in-Christ is none other than *Evangelist Shirley Rice.*

I met Evangelist Rice over ten years ago at Liberty Baptist Church in Gary, Indiana. Liberty Baptist at that time was under the leadership of Pastor Starks, who was a mentor to my Pastor, Lloyd Keith (Mount Hebron MBC), and so Liberty was our Sister Church. We fellowshipped with them annually in celebrating each Pastor's Anniversary in Gary or Chicago. I came to know Elder Rice, not as a Minister, but as a Liberty Choir member. I had no idea she was a minister, nor did she know I was

Evangelist Shirley Rice

a minister also for many years. The reason for this was Rev. Starks did not believe that women should be in ministry or sit in the pulpit. Consequently, when we visited their church, we sang in the combined choirs together, shunned or rejected by leadership - unrecognized as licensed or ordained. When Liberty visited us, if I can recall, she did not sit in our pulpit.

Eventually, my Pastor decided that in order to avoid my feelings being hurt or me being put in a position of feeling uncomfortable, when it was time to be in Gary for Pastor Starks anniversary, I was left behind to conduct the entire service at Mt. Hebron, when the rest of the church would go to Gary. Conducting the whole service was a small consolation prize, as most of the church members would be in Gary. Nevertheless, we had church service with the few who attended those particular Sundays. When her church came to Mt. Hebron, I would see Elder Rice but still had not discovered that her Spiritual gifts and talents were being suppressed. Her humbleness did not allow her to express this to me or disrespect Pastor Starks when visiting, as I could sit in the pulpit at my church. She took her place in the Choir stand and her seat in the Congregation afterward.

Unfortunately, Pastor Starks passed away, and his protégé' Antwon Brown was installed as Pastor. With this transition came a new day, a new dawn. Things changed when Pastor Brown preached for us on the Anniversary of Mt. Hebron. I went into the study and found Elder Shirley sitting in the Pastor's study with the other Ministers, Deacons, and Pastors preparing for prayer. I was surprised to see her sitting there because it had never happened before. I did not question it, I spoke, hugged her, and then Pastor Brown asked if I knew Evangelist Shirley Rice. I was shocked. I said, "Evangelist…you mean all this time?" When we all marched out, I was so happy to escort her to a seat in the pulpit – sitting together. From that moment, Evangelist Rice and I exchanged phone numbers and questioned, "How we didn't know the other existed – in this capacity." She became a source of strength and determination by sharing her journey through ministry – despite adversities.

From that day to this, I can tell you that Evangelist Shirley Rice has been a source of wisdom, inspiration, kindness, and love for me. When I think of her humility, preparedness, and commitment to God and not man, I am inspired. In these past 15 years, I can say that I know when God has sent a guide, a helper, a friend, and a Sister. I consider her a Sister in Christ because she lives out those examples of Christ; she instructs without admonishing, uplifts, and encourages, shows compassion and understanding. My Sister Shirley is a grounded woman in the Word of God that bears no superficialities nor vanity. We began to tell our own stories of strife and struggle in the church's patriarchal settings and lean on and learn from each other.

I have to thank God for Pastor Brown, for he broke the chains of anonymity and allowed my sister to flourish in her rightful place. Elder Shirley uses her platform to bring other women to the forefront to preach, teach, and become an integral part of Church leadership.

I have many reasons to look up to, admire and love this Woman of God; for her purity, her caring soul, her laughter, conversation, guidance, and wisdom. I see and thirst for the Christ in her and pray that some of the anointings would fall on me!

Amber Rice

Amber

I met Dey on the very first day of our middle school year. We were both so young but excited for our future. We sat next to each other on the bus as "skyscraper" by Demi Lovato played over the speaker, which was a song we both liked, we were so nervous to sing in front of each other. She started singing then so did I, after that our friendship was easy. We exchanged numbers and we would talk for hours on the phone then and we still do till this day. We have been friends for over a decade now, which I am so grateful to have a friend like her by my side. Our friendship is something unique that I will cherish forever.

Dey is a very gifted singer. She grew up singing in church and in her moms plays. She was also involved in choir throughout middle school and high school. She has a beautiful voice and a beautiful soul that matches it. Dey is very passionate and will give her all just to see you shine. One of the many things I admire about her. She is a flower that can bloom in the dark places. Throughout high school I enjoyed art and learning about the different mediums of art. I was also involved in different kinds of clubs. The thing we

Dey and Amber

loved to do most was on Friday nights we would go to the football games and have the time of our lives. It's so wonderful to have a christian friend that I can call my Sister In Christ.

We are very different but alike in so many ways but I believe that's how our friendship has lasted this long. We've never let small differences get between our friendship, if anything we learned to love them and which made us stronger. Dey has been there for me from giving me rides to school and till now for being the friend that gives me peace and tranquility. I thank god he has placed such a glorious person in my life in which I will not take for granted.

Annie Davis

Annie

One of my Sisters in Christ is my wonderful sister Laura Dobbs. She has always looked out for me and been there for me since we were little. I remember once when we were kids playing, I fell and hurt my legs. I had sand and dirt all over my legs, and my sister was right there to comfort me. If anyone ever threatened or bullied me, my sister was always there for rescue and protection. When I had my children, I could always depend on her day or night. She is always there to lend a helping hand. In 2006 I was in a car accident and was off work for five months. My super awesome sister was right there for me! I had to go to my Chiropractor appointments from Mondays thru Fridays. I never missed a day, no matter the weather being snow, sleet, rain, or shine. Laura made sure I never missed one appointment! Laura is so special. She cooked meals and made sure I took my medication. I had neck surgery, and my loving, caring sister was there with me every step of the way! When my daughter came home from the hospital with her baby, Laura was right there with her healing hands! She helps to take care of her nephew, fixing meals for him, etc. When my brother was sick, Laura was his caregiver. Laura has been a caregiver since her youth! I am so grateful to call her Sister and "My Sister In Christ!"

Laura Dobbs

Audrey Tolbert

Audrey

Pamela Patterson

My First Lady and Sister Pamela Patterson, whom I can describe as "One Who Lets Her Light Shine." "Let your light so shine before men, that they may see your good works, and glorify your Father which is in heaven." Matthew 5:16. When Reverend and Sister Patterson became part of the Belmount Missionary Baptist Church family, October 2010, they have been a beacon of light uplifting the name of Jesus. Sister Patterson is one whom I can say, has never met a stranger, has a smile on her face, a kind and good-hearted person, and always encouraging others to know that God is in the plan. Sister knows that prayer is the key and faith unlocks the door. Our Sister In Christ Mrs. Pamela Patterson is a blessing to our church family and we love her dearly. We are Sisters In Christ!

Avis (Bubbly) Price

Avis

My best friend is Dorothy Law. I was introduced to her by my rehabilitation counselor. I had been injured and became paralyzed and confined to a wheelchair. Since age 20, my counselor felt that I would benefit from talking to another female who was young and confined to a wheelchair like myself. I did not know anyone else who had suffered a tragedy as I had, and so, I continued with everyday life until I met Dorothy. It was a blessing to meet such an independent woman who was both a wife and a mother. We immediately became Best Friends! We were talking on the phone daily for hours. I learned a lot from Dot. She was married, raised a family, kept her home clean, attended New Revelations Baptist Church, and cooked dinner every day. There was nothing that she could not do because she was in that wheelchair!

What an inspiration Dot is when you witness her in action. We shared all holidays, birthdays, baby showers, childbirths together. We joined a handicapped organization to advocate for the disabled and vacationed in Las Vegas together. She drove a car and picked me up to take me shopping. We prayed together with her mom, who is no longer with us. Mother Tuggle always prayed in the mornings on our morning prayer call. My oldest daughter and Dorothy's son are best friends. She

Avis & Dorothy

has five children, and I have two. We have done soooo much throughout our 47-year friendship that I could write a book alone on it, but I will not do that yet. Thank You, Dorothy, for being my best friend and showing me that there is life after a traumatic injury if you trust in The Lord. He will show you the way.

I WANT TO BE VERY BRIEF IN MENTIONING A FEW WOMEN WHO ALSO HAVE IMPACTED MY LIFE IF I MAY:

Sisters Wilma and Sharon are my sisters from another mother ... Mother Julia Peavy. They are my family. We grew up together in church and spent nights at one another's home. Our mothers were best friends, and our fathers were the Deacons of King Solomon Baptist Church. And now we are Wake Up To Praise Sisters! We are a family over 50 years in the making. Sister Connie "My Twin" from the day I met her at our first retreat, I knew she was special. Her Monday morning messages, and songs of praise are so unique and such a blessing to hear. Lady Pat gave me my nickname (Bubbly) when I met her. Love you.

Elder Shirley who always lifts me up in prayer in the mornings on the prayer line and occasionally blesses us with her amazing voice as well. Spiritual Mother who blesses us with her words of wisdom each week, I Love You. Patty Cakes you are awesome! Sister Claudette, "Island Girl," you are always available for prayer and an encouraging word to lift me up! Your kindness Is contagious! "You are a Rock Star!" Earlean Jordan, thank you for blessing me with a delicious Thanksgiving Dinner every year!

So many others have had such a profound impact on my life. Thank you to all my Wake Up To Praise Family and Friends. 💕 🩶

Sisters in

Carolyn

Carolyn George

Debra Hyatt

I first met this wonderful person Debra Hyatt, in 1981 from dating her brother. She was always so sweet and had such a wonderful personality. Anyone would love her when first meeting her. She was my big sister at that time though I don't think she knew that. I thank her more and more each day for being a part of my family and also for filling my life with all of those colors of happiness and joy. I have so much appreciation as well as thankfulness for her because she has always been such a loving as well as such a caring sister which is more than anyone could ever ask for. We have been through both the good and bad times of life together, yet we weathered the storm. I could not imagine my life without knowing this kind soul. Even to this day, we find ourselves still close to one another and still being supportive of each other. I have always watched her closely because I've learned so much from her over the years. She deserves so much yet ask for so little. If I could have a wish it would be for the angels to grant her all the desires of her heart. Because of her loving spirit, she will always and forever hold a special place in my heart. She is truly my Sister in Christ. I love you Debra Hyatt.

Debra & Carolyn

Clakudette Ayers

Claudette

hat a blessing it has been to have so many beautiful Sisters In Christ throughout my 35 plus years of having a personal relationship with my Lord and Savior Jesus Christ. They have been there for me in just about every season of my life.

I was extremely blessed and fortunate to have had at least ten women I could easily call my Sisters In Christ because of our love and passion for Jesus Christ. However, I would like to highlight two of these women and share my other Sisters In Christ stories in another book. (Smile) I just wanted to let the other Sisters In Christ know that they are very much loved and appreciated. They made my life so much richer by just being there for me through the good, the bad, the ugly, the highs, the lows, and most importantly, the beautiful spiritual moments they chose to share with me. Thank you from the bottom of my heart. So, for this book, I would like to introduce to you Ms. Diane Ayers and Ms. Danita Thomas, my beautiful and amazing Sisters In Christ.

Diane Ayers

Ms. Diane Ayers happens to be both my blood sister and my anointed Prayer Partner. Diane is my older sister, a very loving, caring, devoted, honest sister, mother, grandmother, aunt, cousin, friend, and a dedicated Unit Charge Nurse at Emory Winship Cancer Institute in Atlanta, GA. We both have been serving Jesus Christ for over 35 plus years. We have won many victories along this Christian journey, but there were also times when we had to press in to receive all that God had promised us. I have three other blood sisters, but Diane and I are the closest because of our commitment to Intercessory Prayer for our family and friends, serving at church, love of travel, and love for each other.

Claudette & Diane

I could always depend on Diane to be my Prayer Partner when I needed a strong prayer warrior to stand with me through the years. There were times when we would meet on the phone on a Saturday morning to pray for our family, friends, pastors, church, and the nations. She was in Georgia, and I was in Texas. We saw God move miraculously and answered so many of our prayers. It would always be such a powerful and anointed time of prayer whenever we would get together to pray and worship in person or on the phone. I love to go to God in prayer with Diane because we were always united and focused on defeating our enemies in those moments. That meant the world to me because, in God's remarkable presence, our hearts were overflowing with joy and expectation of how our Heavenly Father was going to answer our prayers. Diane was not only my Prayer Partner, but she was my sister, friend, protector, confidant, one of my biggest supporters, and travel partner.

I remember how much our mother wanted me to go on my first cruise with her, but she passed before I could have gone on that cruise. Diane took the place of Mom when I finally got a chance to go on my first cruise. We had a great time, so I chose this picture taken on that cruise. We are praying that our next trip together will be to Jerusalem to explore and witness where Jesus lived while he was on earth. It will be our first-time visiting Jerusalem, so we are looking forward to that trip.

I can always count on Diane to do the right thing and be ready to give the devil a "black eye" at any moment whenever I asked her to pray "for" me or "with" me. She has such an incredible giving and supportive heart. It is such an honor and joy not only to have her as my blood sister, prayer partner but an amazingly loving Sister In Christ.

The second Sister In Christ, I will share with you is Ms. Danita Thomas. Danita is a Christian Sister I met close to 30 years ago when we worked at Met Life Insurance Company. We instantly connected because of our kindred spirit, passion for Jesus

Danita Thomas

Christ, and our super strong desire to succeed in life professionally. I was always able to talk to Danita on various subjects because of her insatiable appetite to read and absorb lots of knowledge. She was equally willing to share what she had learned with me, which I enjoyed and appreciated very much. Danita is that friend that keeps it real, honest, and enlightening, but she also has a great sense of humor. I can always have belly-aching laughter with her, and negativity was never welcomed into our circle. She is a Bible student, a prayer warrior, and has an incredible talent for creating fun games or being the perfect Hostess. She hosted my Bachelorette Party and did such an excellent job of making sure my guests and I had such a great time. She pulled double duty in 1994 by hosting my Bachelorette Party and being a Bridesmaid.

It was such a joy to have her usher me into this new season of my life. It was so cool that we were not only friends and Sisters In Christ, but we also found ways of being neighbors or roommates. Danita and I are women who know who we are in Christ, what we want out of life, and are willing to work hard to pursue our goals and dreams, but we never competed against each other. We were each other's biggest Cheerleaders depending on whose turn it was to receive the cheers. We always had much love and respect for each other and were willing to support each other's events and endeavors.

Danita, like my Sister Diane, has a heart as big as Texas. She is a tall and pretty native Houstonian who loves her family and friends and would do anything to make their lives better. It is such an honor to be a friend of Danita because it is a relationship where truth, honesty, genuine respect for each other, and the love of Christ are the foundation of our relationship. I respect how she loves and honors her parents, children, grandchildren, family, friends, and co-workers. Whenever I am with Danita, I can be "myself" because she has known me most of my adult life. She has been front and center praying, interceding, standing, and

Danita & Claudette

believing for my victories.

There were times when it appeared that I had lost a few battles, but she was still there, trusting and believing that I will get back on my feet again. Her being there made it more evident that I had won the war, and it gave me such great pleasure to see her standing right next to me. I did not need to say a word; She understood where I had been, where I was at that moment, and she genuinely appreciated the victory God had just given to me. God has clearly shown me how much He affectionately loves both of us. Life had not turned out how we had planned it close to 30 years ago, but our faith has not been shaken, and we are still strong believers in Christ Jesus. We still trust and believe that Our Heavenly Father will complete the good work he had begun in us. We have decided always to pursue the Peace of God.

It is funny that I was there when she became a Flight Attendant for Southwest Airlines almost twenty years ago and when I became a Flight Attendant for Spirit Airlines in 2019, she was right there to show her love and support. I guess that was my way of showing her that I will always look up to her not only professionally but literally (She's 5'8," and I'm 5'2"….LOL.)

Danita and Diane are truly two women who have repeatedly proven that they genuinely cared about me, my life, my future, health, career, and family. I can always count on them being available and present if I need someone to talk to or listen to me. They are there to go to church with, pray with, attend events with, and enjoy an inspirational African movie with me; They enjoy my cooking and takes the time out to visit my beautiful home in Fresno. They allow me to be my best self, and most of all, they are women who genuinely love our Lord and Savior Jesus Christ. It inspires me to see their devotion to serve and obey Christ. They are my accountability partners, and we encourage each other to shoot for the stars. All three of us have been walking with Jesus Christ for an exceedingly long time, but I honestly believe our best is still yet to come.

May God's Amazing Grace, Mercy, Favor, and His Loving Kindness continue to follow My Beautiful Sisters In Christ. I LOVE YOU!!!

Cleopatra Boone

Cleopatra

My Friend/My Sister

SISTER TO SISTER

*Lady Wilma What Is A Friend
and Sister In Christ*

*"A FRIEND IS one of the nicest things
-- YOU CAN HAVE -- and one of the
nicest things -- YOU CAN BE -- our
friendship is "a true blessing to me."*

*Ecclesiastes 4:10 says: If either of
them falls down, one can help the
other up. But pity anyone who falls
and has no one to help them up."*

*Lady Wilma Brumfield-Lofton
and I are like sisters.*

*"SISTER, you are like my angel, with
a love that always glows. You are one of
the greatest my heart will ever know."*

*Proverbs 3:15 says "She is more
precious than jewels, and nothing
you desire can compare with her."*

I met Lady Wilma over a phone conference call that her brother whom I affectionately call Mr. Calvin, invited me to attend. I got a chance to meet this ray of sunshine that I had been speaking to over the phone when she came to Memphis, it was a sad occasion, for her brother's beautiful wife Gloria passed away, we we're at the funeral home and the sun shine walked in and greeted me like she known me all her life, and that's when I nicknamed her "Lady" because of her grace and awesome power to exude love even if you showed dislike. I have never seen such a magnificent presence in my life until I met the Lady behind the voice, and the rest is an awesome fairy tale. She was what Matthew 5: 16 said, "Let your light so shine before men, that they may see your good works and glorify your Father which is in heaven."

She was everything I envisioned in my heart, Lady is simple, no flares about her, everything she does come out of a heart of love. I know from experience my friend/my sister would make a sick person well, because she ministers with her voice, as well as her actions. One scripture says in (KJV) "Yea, a man may say, Thou hast faith, and I have works; shew me thy faith without thy works, and I will shew thee my faith by my works." Wilma does both, and it's all genuine.

Cleopatra & Wilma

I can go on talking about my sister, and it would take a few books, but this Lady has two of the most adorable children, a son and a daughter, three handsome grandboys, and we have the beautiful London who like her great grandma lights up a room, a gorgeous daughter-in-law, an amazing Mother Julia, whom I affectionately call Mom, four darling brothers and a sister by birth, and I am now a part of the Peavy, Brumfield, Lofton family since I got adopted, and I love my adopted family. I believe in my heart of hearts that if I ever needed a hand my adopted family would reach out and grab my hand.

Now my husband, whom she calls her buddy and she is his little sister, and he wants to protect her with his very life because she is such a free spirit who give and loves so freely from the heart, and sees everything in color, she would not, and does not say anything bad about anyone, she has this sweet way of covering everyone with compliments and encouragements making you feel like a King or a Queen. I have a list of about one hundred compliments I can give to my sister, but just these few will do for now. First one, she's always busy, not just for herself, but for everyone else. (2) she has a heart for ministry, and because of that, we have the "Wake Up To Praise" prayer group, we also have "Thursday Night Bible-Study Group." (3) I can call her at anytime, and the sun shines out, she never changes, even in her greeting on her cell phone. I'll stop here, but because of my friend/my sister, I have been a different person, as I try to adopt the sunshine of my sister. I love you beyond tomorrow and back.

I know what Stevie Wonder was saying about you are the "Sunshine Of My Life" but my part to my sister is: "You are the sunshine of my life, and unless death, I will always be around, you are the apple of my eyes, forever you'll stay in my heart." Stay sweet, take care, you are forever covered in prayer.

Scriptures for Prayer and Encouragement

Psalm 34: 10b, Isaiah 26: 3-4; 1 Chronicles 16: 11; 1 John 5: 14-16; 11 Chronicles 6: 21; Jeremiah 29: 11; Psalm 23; Psalm 121; Psalm 91.

Prayer

Father, I ask your blessed covering over my sister, Lord, I block the hearts and minds of those who would try to hurt her, and I decree and declare that she would continually be a blessing to everyone she touches with her hands, her heart and her voice, and always Lord, place the right person in her path every time to be a blessed help for her, both spiritually and most of all financially. This is my prayer to You Lord for her, I am thanking You in advance for the overflow of her blessings even now in Jesus name I pray. Amen and Amen!!!!

Connie "Queen Sparkle" Smith

Connie

A Butterfly Garden

My life is filled with a hue of bright colors in my butterfly garden.

There are flowers that minister to my spirit, flowers that sing, southern bell flowers, sparkling flowers, angel flowers, praying flowers, flowers that reflect son-shine, an American beauty rose, and flowers that wake me up to praise.

As I stroll through my butterfly garden, there is a special flower that calms and gives me expressions of good thoughts. I know I can make it because of this flower; My daughter "Teesa" Michelle.

Michelle "Teesa" Stewart

Oh, look, there in my garden are angel flowers blossoming with flowing petals for all to see. As I continue to stroll, I see glamorous sparkling red flowers, and to my left, my blessed flower. The one that blesses me every day with the unique fragrance of God's love. That flower perfumes the air.

As I look right, my sunny flower is always there as a reminder to thank God for his favor. All my sister flowers inspire my life with their fragrance, beauty, and color.

Each one shows their character in various ways:

My morning flowers wake up with their dew-covered faces smiling at God, and then, the afternoon flowers that speak in soft, fragrant quiet tones of Jesus love for all things.

My evening flowers express the goodness of God. They remind me that He brings sunshine and rain, representing the joy and pain in our lives; we laugh, cry, and grow, knowing in Jesus that we never die.

My night flowers bare the graces of God as they are covered with moonbeams of light; even at night, they show up and show out as it should be, in the moonlight.

Because of God, our Creator, my butterfly flowers are extraordinary in their own way bringing sweet fragrances of insight, beauty, faithfulness, grace, and inspirational colors to other's lives. A spiritual potpourri of flowers to brighten, enlighten, bring peace and joy to my garden. My butterfly garden is filled with my sisters of graciousness, faithfulness, sharing, and caring in God's service.

Patricia "PattyCake" Pittman

All my sister flowers in my garden bless me and other's lives in countless ways.

"Angel" Patricia "PattyCake" Pittman, who I sometimes call (Spiritual Mother Jr.) reminds me of our wonderful anointed friend and Sister In Christ Marietta Jordan. The Spiritual Mother of "Wake Up To Praise," a group of Christian believers that the three of us are members. I met PattyCake about ten years ago on a bible study call. She was introduced to me by Sister Clemmie Kirkwood.

PattyCake is a lady that walks in the grace of God. One of the things that she often says is, "To God Be The Glory!"

We both have grown tremendously in the Lord since joining the WUTP group, lead by Sister Wilma "Lady Sparkle" Lofton. What a blessing! What an experience!

Sister PattyCake expresses Jesus's love in so many ways.

She is a private nurse for children. While she is assigned to one person in the family, the whole family is blessed because blessings follow her. She is like a funnel. The anointing flows in from God through the large end and flows from the smaller end as needed. What a joy she is to be around when we are together, going shopping, visiting, or dropping off gifts to friends; I don't drive. We laugh and sing the Praises of Jesus as we listen to my favorite song called I'm Blessed. We reflect joyously about God's favor and His loving hand in our lives daily. Her greeting to you when asked how are you her reply is "GREATLY BLESSED HIGHLY FAVORED AND DEEPLY LOVED."

She is married to a handsome man of God. PattyCake is the kind of friend you don't mind being with when you would rather be alone. I thank God for blessing my life with a sister of faith as PattyCake. Now can you see she is an up and coming "Spiritual Mother"?

Yes, you are incredibly blessed, highly favored, and so deeply loved. Continue my sweet sister joyfully in God's service, being that one blessing that only you can be in someone's day!!! *Hugs and Smooches* Thankful! Thankful! Thankful! You are My Sister In Christ!

Darcel "Lady D" Strickland

Darcel

I married into a large and loving family. At a family gathering, I met my husband's cousin Shirley Johnson. She invited my family to Reed's Temple C.O.G.I.C., and my son Sean and I went on Mother's Day that year. Were Superintendent David A. Reed is Pastor and overseer. I remember coming into the Blessing Zone with my eyes full of tears, unable to control them. I remember mentioning to Sean that I can not stop crying. I knew then that this church was where God wants me to worship him. Every church member was up on their feet, praising God with everything they had. That made my soul very happy, and I knew that God was pleased with my praising him. The joy of the Lord was with me, even on the ride back home.

Shirley and I were praying on the phone often, and when someone calls us for prayer, we prayed. For a long time, we had been doing that. Until one day, our Pastor put together an Intercessory Prayer Group made up of our church members. Shirley Johnson, Danna Moore, and I prayed every Wednesday at 6:00 AM, and we are still praying even through the Corona virus pandemic. Shirley has been like a sister to me, and she is ready to pray when I need to pray, and when she needs to pray, I am available also. I also pray every Monday at 7:50 AM with Wake Up To Praise with Wilma Lofton. I love Praising our God and his son Jesus Christ.

Darcel & Shirley

Denise Bowling Shaffer

J would like to share all the love and support I received from my Sisters in Christ and the love I have in my heart for these women. My experience in knowing these beautiful women who are truly "Amazing Women."

Many women have done excellently, but I feel these women have surpassed them all. Proverbs 31:29. I will speak on two of these women who have touched my life tremendously. Elder Shirley Rice and Sister Connie Smith, who I feel go above and beyond the call of duty, are unfailing and unlimited in their supply of resources to meet others' needs. I am truly grateful. As a matter of fact, all the women in *My Sisters In Christ* have the same hearts and are there ready to assist and help in times of need. I have my family, which I dearly love, and have had many associates and acquaintances from work in my lifetime, however few I could call friends. According to Proverbs 27:17, as iron sharpens iron, so are my Sisters in Christ. We sharpen the minds of each other as we lift each other in prayer. In our divine connections, God's Word says that two or more are better than one because if one falls, there will be someone to lift that person. My mother, Verlilia Shaffer, passed away June 25th, 2020, early in the morning after being in the hospital for a month battling with COVID; struggling to breathe. Elder Shirley Rice and my Sisters In Christ prayed for my mother around the clock, which brought

Connie Smith

me great comfort. It tore me apart to see my mother struggling to breathe and in such a state of torment and suffering. Her death left me empty, sad, weak, and full of pain. Part of me died along with my mother.

Elder Shirley Rice

Elder Shirley Rice and Sister Connie Smith regularly called me, filling me with God's Word, love, and encouragement. Many other Sisters In Christ sent beautiful cards with words of encouragement and many gifts. I would not be standing tall today if it were not for my Sisters love in Christ. John 15:13 says, "Greater love hath no man or women than this, that a man or women lay down his life for his friends." In Ecclesiastes 4:12, "Though one of us may be overpowered, two can defend themselves, and a two or three-strand cord cannot be easily broken." We submit to the leadership of the Holy Spirit, and we will laugh with those friends who laugh, we will rejoice with those friends who rejoice, and we will weep with those friends who cry. Our prayer for Sisters In Christ is that we can minister to others in love. Lord, by your Holy Spirit, perfect the fruit of our lips. Help us draw thanksgiving forth from the innermost resources; reach deep down into the most secret places of our hearts that we may offer significant thanksgiving to You, Father. In the name of Jesus, I write this letter of appreciation, Amen

Evangelist Denise Moore

I stand in gratitude and awe of the friendship and sisterhood I share with this MIGHTY woman of God. I laugh sometimes because I really can not remember how or where our bond began.

Pastor Taundra D. Williams and I met years ago. We were introduced by her husband, Pastor Lee Williams III. I am not sure if we hit it off right away, but we can all agree that God does ALL things well. Yes, she Pastors (The Launch Church) along side her husband. She wears many hats: Pastor, Mom, daughter, and leader however, I am blessed to call her my sister! We have seen each other through difficult times. We have

Pastor Taundra Williams

laughed, cried, prayed, celebrated, and done it with love and Christ at the center of it all!!

Out of curiosity, I attempted to research the word sister, as you can imagine there were many different definitions for that word. I however have my own. Family is not always blood. My Sister in Christ may not share the same mother, but we definitely share the same father...Jesus!! We are bonded through the Holy Ghost who has made us free to love, encourage, rebuke, and correct each other in the spirit of excellence and meekness. I can be MYSELF with my sister. We can take off the many hats we both wear and just enjoy being women. We are not Evangelist Moore and Pastor Taundra when we are together, we get to enjoy being Denise and Taundra!

Pastor Taundra & Evangelist Denise

In a world of uncertainty I am elated to have my sister with me holding me up, and ready to defend me at the drop of a dime! And the pendulum swings both ways! Don't mess with my girl! Real friendship, and sisterhood will stand the test of time! Cherish the love. What a mighty God we serve!

Joycelyn Tucker

Joycelyn

Although Yvonne and I became friends in high school, it seems that we have known each other all our lives. And I would add that this is one of the attributes that qualify you to be called a Sister In Christ. I cannot remember the exact day and year that Yvonne and I met, but I am sure it was in one of our freshman classes at West Side High School in Gary, Indiana. Of course, I did not know it at the time because I was still a "Babe in Christ," but looking back, I know now that it was The Holy Spirit that brought us together.

I knew many girls in my high school days, but there were very few that I thought of as a friend. I have always been somewhat of a loner, or what people say is a "quiet" person. I have never had a large number of females that made up my inner circle. That was so even when I became an adult. I surmised when I was a teenager that we females can be "messy," "catty," 'jealous," and "vindictive" people; And I never wanted to be like that or have friends who exhibited any of those characteristics.

I had other females in my life who are close to me, but most of them are related by blood or marriage. That is why I know that Yvonne and I are Sisters in Christ because our spirit and character are so much alike in so many ways. I was 'the quiet type,' and so was she. I was not considered to be one of the 'fast girls,' and neither was she. We both come from modest Christian based families. She was a PK (Preacher's kid). And I was a PGK (Preacher's grandkid).

We were both pretty good students academically and socially. I think I am safe in saying that our high school years provided us with many good memories, and upon graduation, we remained very close. I married soon after graduating. Yvonne was my Maid of Honor and hosted my bridal shower. Yvonne married a few years later. Since we had both become wives and mothers caring for our husbands and raising our children, we saw less and less of each other but never completely losing touch with one another down through the years.

Yvonne is a loyal and faithful friend who is like a sister. You do not have to talk to her every-day, week, month, or year to know that she will be there for you whenever you reach out to her, whether it is as simple as chatting to catch up on things or as serious as losing a loved one. That is how I shall sum up my relationship with Yvonne. To further exemplify this, I recall the morning of May 1, 2019, when I rushed to the hospital emergency room to be at my husband's side as he made his transition. Yvonne was one of the first calls I made after I composed myself enough to do so. A short time later, she was walking through the ER room door with her arms open wide. My Sister In Christ!

Julia Peavy

Julia

I have three special women in my life who are like sisters to me. I consider them My Sisters In Christ!

I grew up in Aberdeen, MS as an only child, my mother passed when I was only one month old. My grandmother raised me until she passed, I was six years old. My mother's brother Henry Williams Sr. and his wife my aunt Mary took me into their home and raised me. Uncle Williams and aunt Mary had three children, one girl named Sallie and two boys named Henry Jr. and Benny. My dad Willie Sims, after serving in World War II, married a wonderful woman named Ruby. Dad

Sallie Cook

and Mother Ruby never had any children together which left me as an only child. Sallie is my cousin who I grew up with and she is like a sister to me!

I moved to Chicago, IL when I was sixteen years old and that is when I had the opportunity to spend quality time with my dad and stepmom. Later I married Samuel Peavy who moved to Chicago, IL from Aberdeen, MS a couple of years before I did. In 1951 we moved to Gary, IN. One of my childhood friends Pauline Troope from

Pauline Troope

Aberdeen moved to Gary before me with her husband. Pauline and I stayed in close contact, we would visit each other and we talked almost everyday, we are close like sisters!

In 1955 I met Dorothy Meadows, we lived in the same neighborhood. Dorothy and I became very good friends and still talk several times a week although we live in different states now! It's a blessing to have women in your life who you are able to share the good times and bad times with, you can laugh and cry with no matter the distance you're still just a phone call away to encourage, share ideas, pray for each other and our families! I thank God for friends who are like sisters!

Julia Peavy

Julia

Valla Johnson

Ms. Valla Johnson and I were neighbors for around 30 years. Valla is a person who loves the Lord. She and her husband were a lovely couple and awesome parents. My husband and I enjoyed having such loving, caring neighbors. Both of our husbands loved working in our yards growing beautiful flowers. After our husbands passed, the lawns became our jobs. I even decided to have a vegetable garden which turned out really good. Valla had the most beautiful flowers. Our husbands would be so proud of us! I sold my home and moved to Memphis, Tennessee, but Valla and I still remain in contact with each other. We will always be Sisters In Christ!

LaShonda Haymon

LaShonda

One of my Sisters in Christ is DeLois Jones. We met many years ago, the summer transitioning to 7th grade (although we did not attend the same elementary, middle, or high school), in a summer engineering program. We were wise beyond our years and stayed grounded in gratitude. We lost contact but eventually started working together off and on at a retail store and later on in the optical industry.

LaShonda & DeLois

I am engaged, and she is married with four children, and we keep in touch with one another. We make time to workout together, go shopping, fellowship, etc. We are always there for each other, lending a helping hand when needed, even if that "hand" is just an ear to listen and to provide a testimony of encouragement. I reach out to her for prayer or a shoulder to cry on, and she does the same. I am grateful to have a virtuous, God-fearing Sister in Christ-like her.

LaShonda & Kia

Another one of my Sisters in Christ is Kia Dawson. We met in high school and managed to remain the best of friends ever since. She has the gift of gab and an out-going personality, always willing to help others in need. Although we do not talk every day, we do make time to go shopping, working out, and sometimes take trips together (not since the pandemic, of course). She is an influential, God-fearing, virtuous woman that impact so many people around her.

I once read a quote from an unknown author that states, "Family isn't always blood. It's the people in your life who want you in theirs, the ones who accept you for who you are. The ones who would do anything to see you smile and who love

(L-R) Kia, Genyll, Katura and LaShonda

you no matter what." This quote expresses how I feel about all of my Sisters in Christ; Genyll Hunt, Katura Porter, Erica Gildon, Kelli Hamilton, Chasity Bradley, Ms. Bernice Bradley, the late Kelli Bradley, Daphne Lenoir, Shakira Lenoir, Shekinah Lenoir, and Melvina Dilosa. We are friends that became family surrounded by Christ.

Sisters In Christ are Sisters for Life!!!

LaTasha Sleweon

LaTasha

When I think about Sisters In Christ, I think about friendships and sister bonds that are God's plan. Three individuals come to mind when I think of my sisters in Christ. Those individuals are Tiffany Pitts, Tamia Love, and Abbie Balderas.

I will start with Tiffany since I have known her the longest. Tiffany and I became friends the summer before I began seventh grade when my family moved two houses down from her family's house. Although our friendship had begun, we actually met two years before, when we performed at a music festival. We attended different schools, but at festival practice, her school was seated directly behind my school. She had such a sparkling personality that I remember telling my parents how nice she was, and I did not even know her name. Fast forward, two years later, I was outside playing

Tiffany Pitts

at the new house we moved to, and I looked down the block and saw the girl from the music festival with the sparkling personality. We started playing together and eventually became the best of friends and still keep in touch as adults.

Secondly is Tamia H. She is one of my closest friends. Our friendship started 20 years ago when we became coworkers. Like Tiffany, Tamia and I crossed paths a couple of years

LaTasha & Tamia

before becoming coworkers and friends. I met Tamia while she was working in a store when I was shopping. Tamia's personality also stood out but in a different manner. Fast forward a couple of years when a new employee started working at the store where I worked. When I first saw Tamia at work, I knew there was something familiar about her, but I did not remember why. She and I had very different personalities, and I never thought we would become friends. I could not have been more wrong. A couple of months after Tamia started work, she had some difficult situations take place in her life. That is what made us close. We quickly became friends, and we have been there for each other through some of the best and most difficult times of our lives. We have shared everything from weddings to funerals, childbirth, and childcare. Our children have been friends since they were born. They went to preschool together, have played on some of the same sports teams, and although they are attending different High schools, they will soon be going through the excitement of graduating High school and going to college together.

Last but not least is Abbie B. I recently met her in April of 2019, when we both started cosmetology school. On the first day of class, everyone took turns introducing themselves and telling a little about their self. I soon learned I was the oldest, and Abbie was the youngest, and we had nothing in common, or so I thought, being that she was 20 years younger than me. One day maybe four weeks into cosmetology school, our class had a project in which we were paired up with someone. Abbie's partner did not come to school that day, and my partner was late, so Abbie and I ended up being paired for the project. That project was my first time having a conversation with Abbie. I soon found out how sweet and wise beyond her years this young lady was. Throughout

LaTasha & Abbie

my ten months of cosmetology school, she was my biggest motivator. The day I graduated from cosmetology, she gave me a beautiful letter she wrote about how I motivated her, much to my surprise. I knew that God had placed Abbie and me in each other's lives during that time for a reason. I found out that we were very much alike in many ways; she loves God; she is a hard worker, family-oriented, and has a heart for people.

God put people in your path for specific reasons, no matter if it is an instant friendship, friendships built through situations and circumstances or if the person is half your age. If God wants you all to be friends, you will be friends, and each one of those friendships will be unique in its own way. I know these three ladies are my Sisters In Christ.

Laura Dobbs

Laura

y brother Pastor Taylor Dobbs, married First Lady Michelle 25 years ago after they for dating six years! Michelle is a beautiful s person with a beautiful spirit! It is a blessing to have a sister in law who is a loving, kind and caring person, always there like a sister. Michelle and I love taking about the Lord, we have cried together, laughed together, prayed together and fellowship together. Michelle is certainly My Sister In Christ!

Michelle Dobbs

Lori Strickland

Lori

Relocating to another state and just trying to figure out what's what can sometimes get the best of you. But when it came to meeting a good and genuine person who can take you as you are, meeting Holly was the easy part of relocating! Holly Hogeberg, a fantastic mom, friend, and good person inside and out, became my sister in Christ from her joyful spirit, loving heart, and warm felt words. She has always supported me and has never used a word to tear me down. I am so grateful to have her and her family as a part of me and my daughter's life. I tell her every time we talk, I appreciate her friendship more than anything, and next month we celebrate a five-year string of laughter, love, and good conversations, lol!!

Lori & Holly

Louise Jones

Louise

I've been knowing Sister Jacqueline since 2015. She has been an inspiration to me as I've been to her. We have been sisters in The Sisterhood and missionary for many years.. Jacqueline is a beautiful lady in Christ and I love having conversations with her about the Lord, She is a grandmother again and she really adores her grandchildren! It's so wonderful to have a friend who is close like a sister, we're always there for each other. Our biggest conversation's is about our Lord And Saviour Jesus Christ! One of Jacqueline's favorite sayings is "BUT GOD!" We know God is our everything and we thank God for each other and our Wake Up To Praise Sisterhood!

Jaqueline Gunn

Mary Green

Mary

Sister Clemmie Kirkwood is my Sister In Christ, and we met at church. She is such a kind and caring person. Cracker Barrel is one of our favorite places to have lunch and fellowship together. If I feel down in the dumps, Sister Clemmie is always there to encourage and lift me up! She and Sister Connie Smith conduct a conference call a Bible Study every week teaching God's Word.

I THANK GOD FOR PLACING SISTER CLEMMIE IN MY LIFE!

Clemmie Kirkwood

Pastor Mary Spratt

"Women of God Committed to the Call"
A Short Narrative by, Elder Mary Spratt

When times are tough, sometimes we need an encouraging voice or uplifting story to help get us through. That's why we've collected a few of our favorite, uplifting, laugh-out-loud stories to bring you comfort, and to remind you that we're in this together.

Looking back on my life I understand that my childhood memory played a big part of forming my character. It is amazing to me that such a short span of my life affected many phases of my adult life…good and bad.

I was raised in a family of twelve people. I had 1 father and mother, (some children have more), six brothers, and six sisters. Living in a large family can have its challenges, but for some reason we survived them all, which is amazing because we only had three bedrooms, and for a longtime outside toilets, no TV, and no telephone until I was twelfth grade. But we were committed to each other, whatever we had we were taught to share until everyone got a bite of the pie, and We were all so happy, as of today the twelve beautiful children that God blessed my parents to birth into this great world, we are All still living to share our story, we had very little but God made what we had much, because my parents placed it in God's mighty hands.

My parents were committed. They were married for many years until death separated the two, and truly loved and enjoyed one another. Oh…they had some tough times, but commitment goes deeper than tough times. Commitment is a state of mind. As I began my adult life my childhood life stories have been much support to my adult life, I've had to use so many things that I learned from my mother and grandmother on my adult journey, Commitment have gotten me to this place in my life, My Christian journey began when I was a young lad but I had very little understanding at this time what God was preparing for my life, but as I kept the course I begin to learn more and more about this Christian walk, and it all started with me being a Missionary at a very young age but was unaware in my own neighborhood, I would perform many duties for the elderly involving cutting their lawns, gathering wood, cooking, washing, personal care and whatever else they needed that I was big enough to do, Now God have place greater works upon me to go forth like a mighty roaring lion.

Later on, on my Christian walk God sent two great God-fearing women into my life and we connected and became best friends, as well as great missionaries around Northeast Mississippi to do mission work great and small.

GOD FEARING WOMAN

Alma Williams

I Missionary Alma Williams, A Mother of three daughters, and five grandchildren. As being a missionary God let me know that I had a work to do, and as time went by.

In 2004 my husband was diagnosed with a form of cancer known as Hodgkin's Lymphoma. As a wife, your heart aches when your spouse is sick. It devastated me to see my husband suffer with such overwhelming sickness. But I knew that I could go to God in prayer. Through God's grace and mercy, that day I was not only his wife but I became his personal nurse and caregiver. There were nights that I found myself crying out to God, praying that he would heal my husband. I went to the Father, interceding on my husband's behalf. God not only heard my prayer but he answered it also. My husband through the healing of the Lord is still here telling his testimony of God's healing power. I really had to call on the Lord Jesus Christ, As I prayed and ask my prayer warriors to touch and agree with me in prayer' God let me know that everything would be alright'.

About ten years later after my husband's battle and healing with cancer, in 2014 my daughter was diagnosed with non-Hodgkin Lymphoma. As a mother, it breaks your heart to see your child sick with such debilitating sickness. I found myself pleading and interceding on my daughter's behalf. On this day I was not only her mother but I became her nurse and personal caregiver. I prayed to God. The people of God prayed to God. God didn't just hear our prayer but he answered our prayer also and my daughter is still here telling her testimony of God's healing power. God continues to show himself faithful. When you pray to God, you know that God hears you. Because you know that God hears you, you know your prayers are answered.

Each time, I called on the prayer warriors to pray and they did just that'. I thank God that through prayer and the Holy Ghost God healed my husband and my daughter. God also gave me the grace and strength to endure. Although the responsibility was great, God never left me. Through the Word of God, I remained encouraged.

Whatever you are going through let us always give God the glory, because all the glory belongs to Him.

Missionary Alma Williams

Annie Davies

And I, Missionary Annie Davis, the Mother of one daughter, and two granddaughters, I answer my call to go forth in Missionary field, it's a great area of work, but some count it as lows degree, but God counts it as a high level of degree. The two wonderful ladies that you have read about in the above narratives are truly sent by God to do what they do, many people have been delivered and heal through our Christian journey, we connect in the spirit of God, we pray, shop, dine, read, sing, cry, talk, worship and encourage each other at all times together. As the scripture says in, Matthew 18:20, For where two or three are gathered together in my name, there am I in the midst of them. The Mission work have gone from disturbing food to the homeless and the elderly, visit the sick and shut-in, various hospital, beavered families, lost of employment and whatever the need maybe we try to take care of it. We are willing to do God's will because that is our desire that God will continue to pour out his anointing upon us each day, so many people is hurting and just sometimes need and encouraging word at time, its our aim to be there for God's people when needed. God honor a cheerful giver at all times. We as missionary carry the work God have assigned to our hands even deeper, if our children fall in a crisis, we are there for them no matter the distance day are night we will rise up out of ours beds to go to them and meet the needs that have occurred. The bible says in Revelation 2:29, He that hath an ear, let him hear what the Spirit saith unto the churches." And we as Christian Women on the move For God We desire to have a listening ear to hear what God is saying to us. Lord, please continue to use Us because we don't mind to "Wake Up the Praise"

Missionary Annie Davis

Annie, Pastor Mary & Alma

Nell Totten

How We Met!

ow, it seems like Pat and I have been friends forever. Actually, friends are not an accurate way to describe our relationship, for we are family, not like family, but family. I met Pat at a point in my life where God was already dealing with me to get my life together; I just did not even know where to begin. I had left a very promiscuous life in my small town. I decided to move to Memphis to go to school and further my education so I could have a different life. I just did not know how to accomplish this; I just knew I wanted to change.

Then I met Pat. She, too, had just moved to Memphis. Her husband was pastoring a new church there, a Pentecostal church, something I did not know about or even understood. What struck me first was her smile. It was genuine – not fake. She was very quiet at first, but I later learned that quiet was not Pat. She is very opinionated. Vocal but usually right.

Cleopatra Boone

You see, Pat was "saved," which was a term I did not understand. It was an identity to her, and I could not relate to it. Yes, I was raised in the church and had a Godly grandmother, who went to heaven when I was 9. But other than that, I had only been exposed to the concept that you make a "profession of faith," do what you want to do, and you were still going to heaven. So being saved was not a big deal to me. Pat was different. Other people noticed it too, ha-ha, that is how we became friends, she was "too saved" for the other ladies in the classroom, and oddly enough, I was "too white." We both were the odd man out when it came to friendships in our small class. Remember, this was the early 80's.

This journey began back in 1983 and has been quite an experience that I really have gleaned from; our friendship saved and changed my life.

First, we just were school friends, you know the regular stuff, sat together in school, ate lunch together, and studied together. Then one day, Pat told me, yep, told me, it was a command, "You are going to church Sunday, be ready, my husband will be picking you up." Her tone did not leave room for discussion; it was going to happen. And happen it did. The Pastor came by and picked me up. Now you got to understand, this was in the early '80s, and I looked out the window and saw the biggest black man I had ever seen in a car waiting for me. I was scared to get in but also scared not to. Pat said, "you are going to church," and she was serious. Well, my fear was short-lived. The Pastor was so nice and immediately took on the role of Papa to me, something I never had, and it was amazing; it gave me value and love. Pat opened me to a whole new world of "Christian folks" and being loved in the relationship in the body of Christ.

In those early years of friendship, Pat really took on the role of mama to me. She taught me how to dress, taught me how to have good hygiene, cook, clean, all the things that a good mom would teach her child. You see, I was raised by an alcoholic mom and did not get any of this training, so at 20, I was a real mess!

I wish I could say I was a good friend back, but I was not. I wish I could say I was a perfect Christian because of our friendship, but I was not. In fact, being such a mess, it has taken me years to learn some of the lessons that Pat tried to teach me during my early twenties. I have learned that being "saved" is a lifelong commitment because of our friendship. It's making a decision every day to serve the Lord and others. I remember when Pat decided that I needed to learn how to dress, she opened her closet and dressed me. This was not charity work. This was a friend, a sister helping another friend/sister learn how to respect herself by teaching her to dress correctly and dress with value and purpose. Pat freely opened her own personal closet and dressed me. As I have gotten older, I realize how big that really is. How Christ-like, to take care of another person, especially when you are struggling to have something. As I have gotten older, I realize Pat reached out in friendship and love, despite our own circumstances and needs. During those early years of friendship, I thought Pat "had it all together" she was always so confident and bold. But as I am going through situations and maturing, I realize that she was trying to survive and maintain herself and reach out to me. Wow, that is big, to really think about someone making a decision to "be saved" every day, working through ministry, family, marriage, work, and still reaching out and helping me. I am forever grateful.

Well, I will end this on this note. When I say that Pat has had the most impact on me during my adult life, I am really serious. You see, typically, alcoholic parents produce alcoholic children; that is a proven statistic. Family curses are real, and for all reasons, I should be following that cursed path. I am not, because of Pat's friendship and the path she led me to – the way to Christ, being "saved." I am saved today. My husband and I have a beautiful children's ministry, where we teach about Christ, but we teach our young people that they have value and purpose in God's Kingdom. We feed, clothe, and get involved in our young people's lives – leading them to Christ. This is genuinely the fruit of Pat's Christian labor from 40 years ago. In fact, she has met our children and her husband, Pastor Boone, married my husband and me several years ago at our little church. Talk about coming full circle.

All of this is because of Jesus, but on this earth, we are His hands and feet, and I, especially as I get older, chose daily to be "saved," to love despite my situations of life, to reach out to young people, and point them to Christ. Just as my friend-sister did to me many years ago.

Sharon Haymon

Sharon

When I was asked to pick a Sister to write about, I thought about every one of my Sisters from Wake Up To Praise, making it difficult to pick just one. We are all GOD'S Children!!! Being a part of Wake Up To Praise and coming together every Monday morning on one big prayer line allows me and others to fellowship with so many different people, mainly women, all over the United States. You began to feel the love, compassion, and admiration for every caller on the line. You learn a little bit about them, and they learn a little bit about you. We laugh together, cry together, pray, and support each other. I feel closer to some of my WUTP Sisters than I am with friends I have known all my life. That is saying a lot about the character of my WUTP Sisters. They are just good, faithful, GOD fearing, loving, caring, spiritual, beautiful, praying, and phenomenal women of GOD!!! How blessed are we to have each other?

My Sister Wilma Lofton has always been there for me down through the years. I can talk to her about anything. She is very Spiritual and wise and always gives good advice.

My Sister In Christ, Elder Shirley Rice, is another very spiritual woman I love and enjoy talking to. She makes you feel so good and confident after speaking with her.

Then there is My Sister In Christ, Lady Pat, who always makes your day and sends you on a spiritual journey with daily uplifting text messages.

My Sister In Christ Connie Smith, who always put an

uplifting song in your heart and soul.

And our Spiritual Mother Marietta Jordan, whose spirit-filled spoken message on Monday mornings graces the innermost layer of your soul. She is truly one of a kind.

And our fired up for Jesus, My Sister In Christ Lady Pattycake, when she speaks of the goodness, greatness, and mercy of Jesus and all He has done for us, you can feel the fire in your soul. She is more spiritual, powerful and anointed than she knows.

Then there is my Sister In Christ, Avis Price, a beautiful person I have known for many years. She always gives good advice and is so easy to talk to.

And My Sister In Christ Lady "D" Darcel Strickland, another beautiful and spiritual woman I have known for many years. She prays for everyone and loves to see people happy.

And my cousin and Sister In Christ Louise Jones, whom I just learned is my cousin since WUTP started. Louise is very spiritual, and she is always trying to help someone. I enjoy talking with her. We have a lot in common. No wonder we are cousins (smile).

Also, our Island Girl, Sister In Christ Claudette Ayres. She is a very spiritual hard-working, dedicated Sister who loves the Lord, prays, cares for others, knows what she wants in life, and knows how to get it. She is definitely a go-getter.

Sammye Clemons

I can go on and on about the beautiful, dedicated, loving, caring, spiritual Sisters of WUTP, each one as loving and caring as the next. It is almost impossible to pick or choose one person from our WUTP family. So, the Sister that I have chosen is a Sister that I just met about a month ago, over the telephone, when my husband was sick. She knew my family members, but she did not know me, and I did not know her, but she called me every week to tell me that she is praying for me, my husband, and our entire family. She wanted us to know that GOD loves us and if there was anything that she can do for us, to let her know. She told me I was welcome to call her anytime. I felt genuine compassion, Godliness, and friendship from this person that I did not even know. This is how GOD wants HIS Children to treat each other. Her name is Sammye Clemons, and she is an excellent example of GOD's Love that is why she is My Sister In Christ.

Sharon Haymon

Sharon

I have known my mother-in-law, Mother Evelyn Haymon for many years and she has always inspired me. She, my father-in-law, husband, and I used to go out to dinner, bowling and to baseball games together. We would have lots of fun. They were so young at heart and full of energy. When my husband and I got married, I started calling her Mother Evelyn. I wanted to call her Mother Haymon, but that was my grandmother-in-laws name; so, to make it less confusing, I started calling her Mother Evelyn.

Mother Evelyn Haymon

She really loves the LORD! She is the Church Mother of Williams Chapel in Gary, Indiana under Pastor Anthony Williams. She is the Matriarch of the Haymon Family and a true Prayer Warrior. She has prayed our family through some rough and turbulent times, through sickness, childbirth, surgeries, bad accidents, cancer, kidney transplantation, COVID and so much more and each situation turned out wonderful, healthy, and fine. GOD is good all the time! She is the mother of 7 children: William Jr., Howard, Kathy, Danny, Lisa, Jerry and Tony. She and my father-in-law, William Haymon Sr., have been married for 64 years. They were made for each other. I love the way they do everything together, go to church, shopping, out to dinner and they enjoy watching movies and old westerns together. Mother Evelyn is always so willing to lend a helping hand. If I needed her for anything, she would be right there for me or anyone else in her family. She loves her family, and we love her. I definitely consider Mother Evelyn Haymon my Sister In Christ.

Sharon & Evelyn

Sharon Haymon

Sharon

I have several friends that I have known since high school. They are Patricia Henderson Parker, Marella Chamberlain, Shirley Clark Baity and one friend that I have known since 7th grade name Sabrina Morris. Each one of my friends are kind, loving, and loves the Lord.

We do not see or talk to each other as much as we would like but, when we do it is like time stood still just for us. We reminisce and talk for hours and hours. Every once in a while, we get together on girl's night out. We talk, have fun, and remember "the good ole school days." It is long overdue!

We have not talked to our friend Patricia in many years, because we lost contact with her. We are all friends and I know she thinks of us just as much as we think of her. Best friends are always close in heart even though we are apart. These ladies are, and always will be, My Sisters In Christ.

Shirley Clark Baity

Marella Chamberlain

Sabrina Morris

Tawana Clemons

Tawana

What can I say about my Sister In Christ/Life, Kiva Mallory? Ecclesiastes 4:12 says it best. "Though one may be overpowered, two can defend themselves. A cord of three strands is not quickly broken!"

Our friendship was nowhere traditional. I met Kiva four years ago when I was in a very low place in my life. I had just moved to Memphis and had to have emergency surgery. Afterward, I had to miss a month off work, and my job was threatening to fire me. Kiva never gave up on me or my mental state of mind. I am used to being a blessing. So, it was hard to receive HELP if you know what I mean. But, she would never give up on me. She was always there with uplifting words, gas money, a shoulder to cry/lean on. Needless to say, she is my Proverbs 31 woman since our meeting

Kiva & Tawana

four years ago. We are now Church members, and she has written a book called Sisters Let's Chat. And, greatest of all, she has become a grandmother. I am so grateful for my LIFE SISTER... The word says"Iron sharpens Iron" and that she did. I love you to life. Thank you for being a friend!

Virginia Maddox

Virginia

*S*isterhood, sister-friend, sister-ship, or just plain Sister are the descriptions I think about when I think of Alice Williams and Prophetess Eloise Hinton. One definition for sisterhood is loving and accepting someone where they are but consistently inspiring them to their highest potential and God's will for their life—moving on to sister-friend. Urban Dictionary says that sister-friend is a person who is always there for you. Similar to a best friend but more, someone you hope will be in your life forever. Your bestest friend. Better than a friend. Sister-ship, one who in the role or position of a sister. I met Alice Williams first and Prophetess Eloise Hinton later.

I will begin here by talking about my journey with Alice Williams.

In the early eighties, I worked for the US Government, in the Intelligence organization, at Redstone Arsenal in Huntsville, Alabama, when I met Alice Williams. We became friends and prayer partners. We spent many of our lunch hours praying together, petitioning God with our prayer lists. Alice and I joined the same church and were also members of the young adult choir. Alice had four sons, and I had two daughters and a son. Our families spent Holidays together and shared many pot-luck suppers too.

We usually started our day attending early Morning Prayer at 5:00 A.M. at the church. We have Prayed together,

Alice Williams

witnessed to many people about our Lord and Savior Jesus Christ. Alice is my Sister in Christ. She has witnessed to my family, and I have witnessed to her family too.

Throughout the years, we have prayed together and encouraged each other in the Lord by having bible studies, sharing God's Holy Bible, sharing the Gospel of Jesus Christ, and leading and reconciling others to God. We have also had all night prayer meetings in our homes and in the church too. I still thank God for sister-ship and our sisterhood and often reflect over the many prayers that we petitioned God for and how he answered them. He did answer them, some not in the way we prayed He would. Most of them were answered with a yes from Him, some of them a no, not the way we wanted them answered, but He heard them and answered us in His perfect will. We believe in carrying everything to God in Prayer, asking Him in the Name of Jesus. No matter what the problem or the petition, we ask God for His directions and protection. Above all things, we give Him all the Praise and Thanksgiving because He is worthy to be honored and Praised. I also thank God for my sisterhood journey with Alice, He knew that I needed an earthly sister that loves Him, so I believe He allowed our paths to cross.

The next Lady that I want to introduce you to is Prophetess Eloise Hinton.

Prophetess Eloise Hinton

The above sisterhood, sister-friend, and sister-ship definition applies to her too. I met Prophetess Hinton in the mid-nineties at the church we attended together. We were a member of the Prayer Warriors' Team and would meet at Noon to pray at our church. Prophetess Hinton and I became friends, she always encourages me, and we also pray together. She is the Elder of our church, where her son-in-law and daughter are Pastors. Our Sisterhood Journey has made us realized that God is only a prayer away. We stand on Matthew 18:18-19. "Verily, I say unto you. Whatsoever ye shall bind on earth shall be bound in heaven: and whatsoever ye shall loose on earth shall be loosed in heaven. Again, I say unto you. That if two oh you shall agree on earth as touching anything that they shall ask, it shall be done for them of my Father which is in heaven." That God works suddenly in some situations and others, He will be there, right on time. Prophetess Hinton has been and is a caregiver for her siblings; like I was the sole caregiver for my Mother. We understand the dependence of others that needs help. We are there for them and helping them along the way. She loves the Lord, has a heart of gold, and is very kind. I thank and praise God for our Sisterhood, Sister-friend, and Sister-ship.

The two Godly women that I have shared with you are like sisters to me. I have three brothers, and I am the only female. These two ladies are the sisters I never had. Their goals are the same as mine. To build up the Kingdom of God and lift-up the Name of Jesus on the highways and bi-ways; Notifying the world that there is no other name on earth or in heaven whereby men can be saved but the name of JESUS.

Wanda Davis

Wanda

*I*t gives me such great pleasure to mention this beautiful friend and mentor -Suave, Sophisticated, God-fearing Woman of God, Banker, and my sister Sales Associate, Selena Craft Williams. She has shared the ups and downs of life with me along life's tedious way. We both lost our wonderful husbands. I shared with her in her loss (Sung at her husband's homegoing), and she shared with me in my husband's homegoing. Lastly, I had to transition to another resident. Moving was one of the most upsetting parts of my life because I had raised my family in that home for 30 years, but Selena was right there knocking on my door with a financial solution. Little does she know that I have labeled her my Friend, Mentor, and Sister In Christ! I Love You, Dearly

Thank You

A special thank you to our Wake Up To Praise family and all of our friends who shared their stories.

TO GOD BE THE GLORY